MW00905392

EXPLORING OCEANS

Nicholle Carrière
Genevieve Boyer

Contents

Exploring the Oceans

The Earth's oceans have always been mysterious. Life there is very different than it is on land, and so are the plants and animals.

Most of life on Earth is aquatic, meaning "living in the water." Scientists think there may be 25 million different kinds of plants and animals that live in the ocean.

Oceans of the World

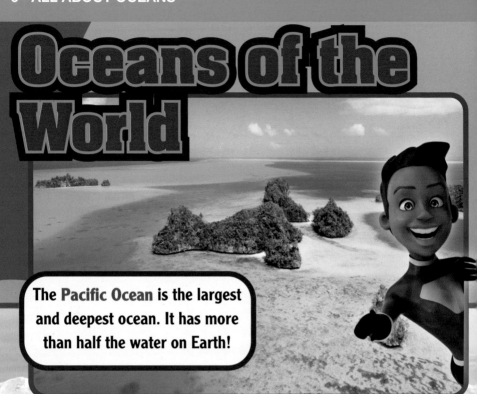

The **Pacific Ocean** is the largest and deepest ocean. It has more than half the water on Earth!

Polar Bears

The **Atlantic Ocean** is the second largest ocean. The currents in the ocean water create a lot of the weather in the eastern United States and Canada, especially hurricanes.

The **Indian Ocean** is between Africa and Asia and the Antarctic Ocean. Many important transportation routes go through this ocean.

Sea Turtle and Fish

The Arctic and Antarctic Oceans are at the North and South Poles. They are the smallest oceans and have the coldest water.

Penguins

A Look at Salt Water

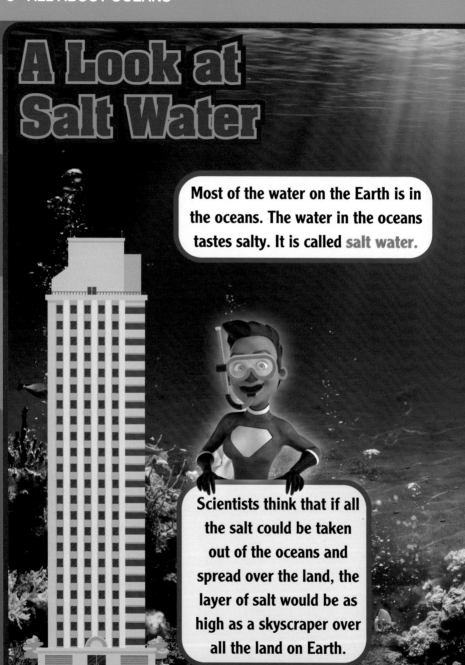

Most of the water on the Earth is in the oceans. The water in the oceans tastes salty. It is called salt water.

Scientists think that if all the salt could be taken out of the oceans and spread over the land, the layer of salt would be as high as a skyscraper over all the land on Earth.

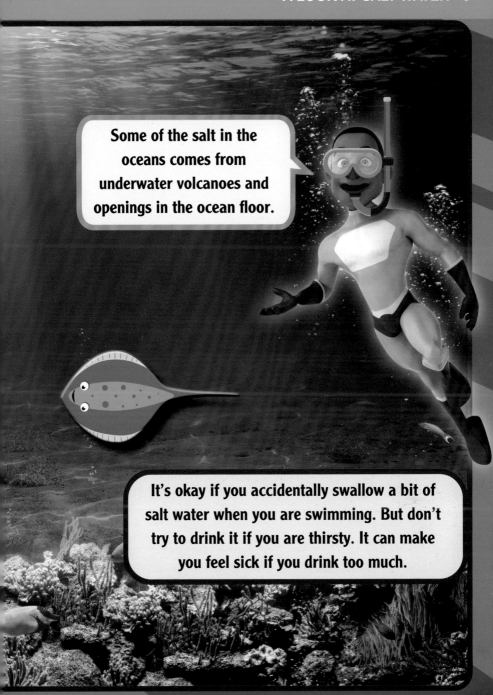

Some of the salt in the oceans comes from underwater volcanoes and openings in the ocean floor.

It's okay if you accidentally swallow a bit of salt water when you are swimming. But don't try to drink it if you are thirsty. It can make you feel sick if you drink too much.

Ocean Zones

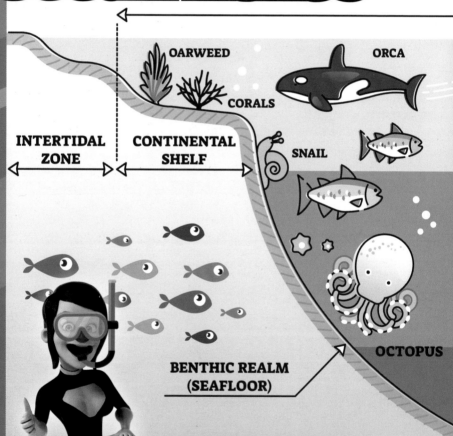

Different plants and animals are found in different parts of the ocean. Some prefer to live near the surface where there is a lot of sunlight. Others live in the deepest parts of the ocean where there is no light at all!

PELAGIC REALM

0 m

PLANKTON

JELLYFISH

WHALE SHARK

200 m

SPERM WHALE

APHOTIC ZONE

TWILIGHT

LEATHERBACK TURTLE

1000 - 4000 m

GULPER EEL

SPONGE

ANGLERFISH

NO LIGHT

PHOTIC ZONE

SEA CUCUMBER

6000 - 10000 m

Ocean Currents

Arctic Ocean

North America

Atlantic Ocean

South America

Ocean currents are flows of seawater. Currents can be warm (red on the map) or cold (blue).

Pacific Ocean

 warm currents ● cold currents

Antarctica

The wind causes surface currents. These currents travel clockwise in the Northern Hemisphere and counter-clockwise in the Southern Hemisphere.

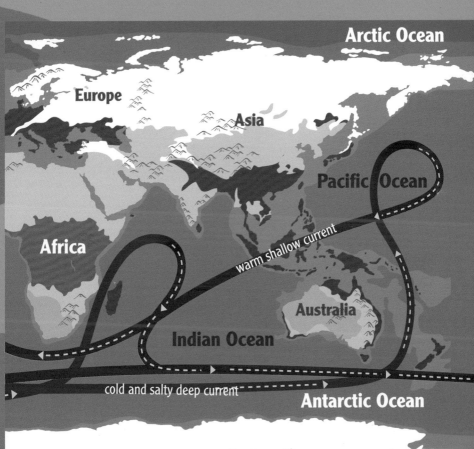

Arctic Ocean

Europe

Asia

Pacific Ocean

warm shallow current

Africa

Australia

Indian Ocean

cold and salty deep current

Antarctic Ocean

Antarctica

Open Ocean

More than half the ocean environment is, open ocean. It is the part of the ocean away from land.

Whales and other big sea creatures live in the open ocean. So do sea turtles and many kinds of fish. The ocean waters are full of life!

Humpback Whale

Many tiny creatures like, plankton, shrimp and krill, also live in the open ocean. They are food for larger animals.

Plankton

Frogfish

The deepest parts of the ocean are dark and cold. The creatures that live there are strange, and scientists don't know much about them.

The Ocean Floor

Scientists can map the ocean floor using images from satellites or by using sound waves to measure depth.

Mid-ocean Ridge

The ocean floor is full of life. You can find **coral reefs** full of fish, anemones, sea slugs and other creatures. Octopuses and eels live in rocky outcrops. Kelp forests are rooted in the ocean floor.

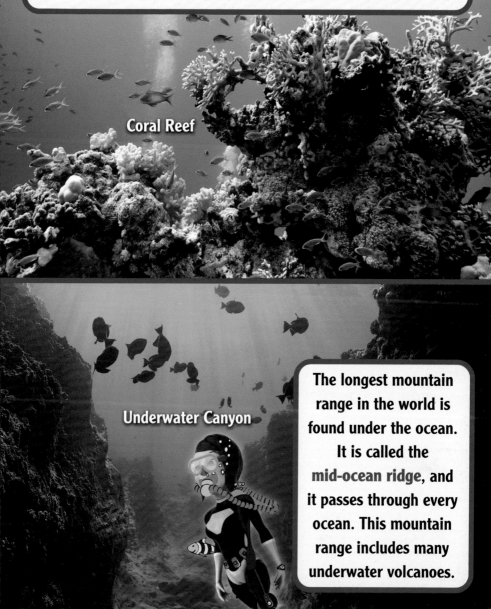

Coral Reef

Underwater Canyon

The longest mountain range in the world is found under the ocean. It is called the **mid-ocean ridge**, and it passes through every ocean. This mountain range includes many underwater volcanoes.

Deep Sea

Scientists used to think that nothing lived in the deepest parts of the ocean. There isn't any light, and it's very cold. What could live there?

Ghost Fish

They were surprised to find that many strange creatures live in the ocean depths. Some, like the ghost fish, have no color and eyes like mirrors so it can see in the dark.

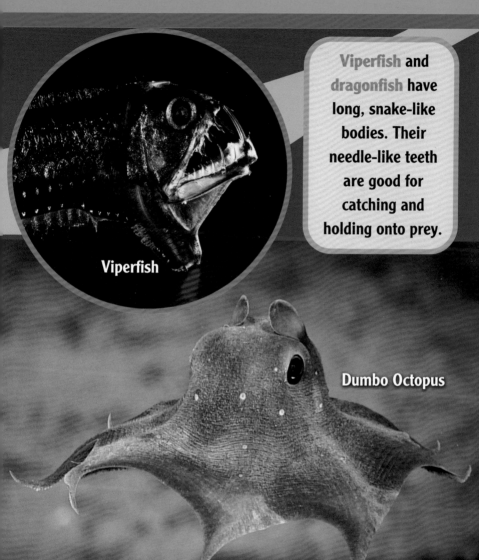

Viperfish and dragonfish have long, snake-like bodies. Their needle-like teeth are good for catching and holding onto prey.

Viperfish

Dumbo Octopus

Dumbo octopuses live deeper in the ocean than any other octopuses. They use their fins (which look a bit like Dumbo the elephant's large ears!) to move forward. They use their long arms to steer.

Icebergs

Icebergs are giant pieces of ice floating in the ocean. You can see them in the North Atlantic Ocean and the Antarctic Ocean.

Most of an iceberg is under the water. Only a small part sticks up out of the water.

Icebergs are chunks of ice that break off glaciers, ice shelves or bigger icebergs.

The ocean close to the South Pole has huge icebergs. The biggest one is called A-76. It is about the same size as Prince Edward Island in Canada.

Underwater volcanoes form from cracks or holes in the ocean floor. Most are found in the mid-ocean ridge.

These volcanoes are also called seamounts.

Underwater Volcanoes

Lava erupts from these volcanoes. The lava sometimes comes to the surface and forms islands, like the Hawaiian Islands in the Pacific Ocean and Surtsey Island near Iceland.

There are about 1500 active volcanoes on the Earth's surface, but more than 10,000 underwater volcanoes just in the Pacific Ocean!

Hydrothermal Vents

Super-hot water flows from hydrothermal vents that are openings in the ocean floor. These vents often occur near underwater volcanoes.

The water temperature at these vents can range from 140°F (60°C) to 867°F (464°C). Water boils at 212°F (100°C). That's really hot!

Tube Worm Colony

Some plants and animals, like snails, tube worms and barnacles, can live near the vents!

Crabs and Mussels

Kelp Forests

Kelp is a kind of seaweed. Beyond the shoreline, kelp forests are home to many different animals.

These large seaweeds have gas-filled sacs on their leaves. The sacs help the plant stay upright in the water.

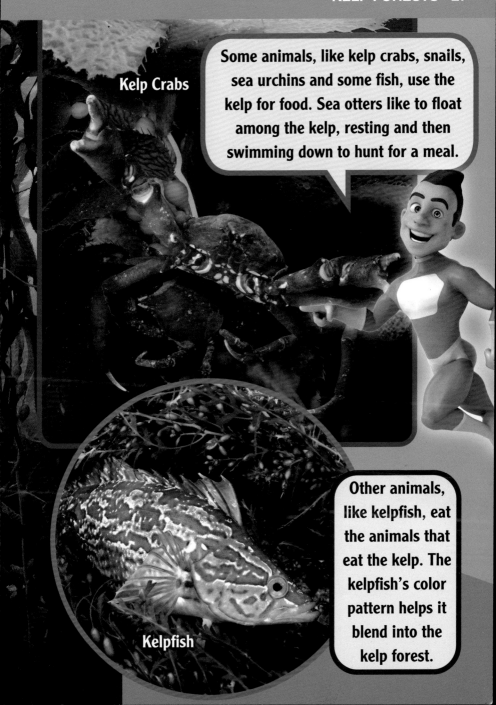

Kelp Crabs

Some animals, like kelp crabs, snails, sea urchins and some fish, use the kelp for food. Sea otters like to float among the kelp, resting and then swimming down to hunt for a meal.

Other animals, like kelpfish, eat the animals that eat the kelp. The kelpfish's color pattern helps it blend into the kelp forest.

Kelpfish

Coral Reefs

Coral reefs are home to an amazing variety of marine animals. Coral reefs are usually found in warm, clear, shallow water.

Sea Fan Coral

Corals are made by groups of small animals called polyps. They build a hard exoskeleton around themselves.

Coral Polyps

Pillar Coral

Brain Coral

Coral reefs are a habitat for many kinds of fish and other sea creatures. Plants grow among the coral, too. Coral reefs are an important part of the ocean environment.

Plankton

Plankton

Plankton are tiny plants and animals that live near the surface of the ocean. They don't swim. They just drift in the water.

Plankton are an important food for many fish. Even huge whales eat plankton!

Daphnia

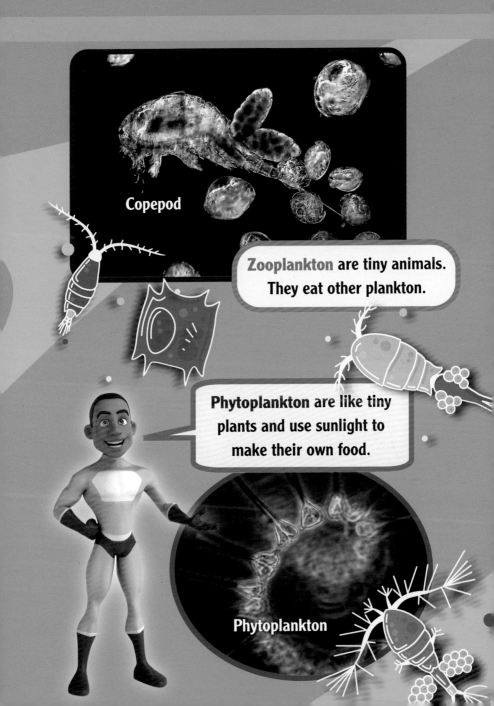

Copepod

Zooplankton are tiny animals. They eat other plankton.

Phytoplankton are like tiny plants and use sunlight to make their own food.

Phytoplankton

Sea Urchins

Sea urchins are round, spiny animals. The spines can move and point in any direction.

Sea Urchin

Urchin Beak

Sea urchins have five sharp teeth on the bottom of their shell and a fleshy tongue. They eat algae, plankton, barnacles and dead fish.

Purple Sea Urchins

Burrowing Urchin

Sea urchins live in every ocean and at different depths. Some live in shallow water near the shore. Others live in the deepest parts of the ocean.

Seashells

Seashells

Seashells are made of calcium carbonate, the same mineral that eggshells and coral are made from.

Clam

Many seashells are bivalves. These shells have two identical halves joined by a flexible hinge. Clams, mussels, scallops and oysters have bivalve shells.

Whelk Shells

Other sea creatures have single, often spiral shells. These include sea snails, nautiluses and conches.

Limpets and Barnacles

Limpets and barnacles have cone-shaped shells.

Sea Stars

Purple Sea Star

Sea stars, also called starfish, are not really fish. They are related to sea urchins, sand dollars and sea cucumbers. Many sea stars have five arms, but some kinds have 10, 20 or even 40 arms!

If a sea star loses an arm, it can grow a new one! This is called regeneration.

Sea Star

Sea stars move using tiny tube feet on the underside of their bodies. With its 15,000 tube feet, the sunflower sea star moves the fastest but can only go slightly faster than a snail!

Sea Star Feet

Sunflower Sea Star

The sea star uses its suction-cupped tube feet to open clams and oysters. Then its stomach comes out of its mouth and surrounds the prey. After the prey is digested, the sea star pulls its stomach back into its body.

Jellyfish

Jellyfish have been on Earth for 600 million years! That's even before dinosaurs! Some jellyfish are bigger than a person. Others are so small that they are hard to see.

Medusa

Box Jellyfish

The Australian box jellyfish is the most venomous sea creature on Earth.

Orange Jellyfish

Jellyfish don't have a brain, blood, bones or a heart! But they can detect light, vibrations and chemicals in the water.

The lion's mane jellyfish is the biggest jellyfish. It can be more than 7 feet (2.1 m) wide, and its tentacles can be more than 120 feet (37 m) long. That's longer than a football field!

Lion's Mane Jellyfish

Anemones

Green Anemone

Anemones look like flowers, but they are really animals. Most anemones attach themselves to rocks, but some burrow into sand or gravel on the ocean floor.

Orange Anemone

You can find anemones all over the world. They can be as small as your fingernail or as wide as a person is tall. The most colorful anemones are found in tropical oceans.

Anemones have many **tentacles** around a small mouth. When a fish swims past, the tentacles shoot it with a paralyzing poison. Then the tentacles guide the helpless fish into the anemone's mouth.

Tiger Anemone

Clownfish are immune to the anemone's poison. They can live safely among the tentacles, which protect them from predators.

Clownfish in Anemone

Crabs

Violinist Crab

Rainbow Crab

Crabs are **decapods**, which means they have 10 legs. Two of the legs are claws. Crabs walk and swim sideways.

Crabs have a hard outer shell called an **exoskeleton**. It protects the soft tissue inside. Their shells are made of **chitin**.

Japanese Spider Crab

The largest crab is the **Japanese spider crab.** It measures about 12 feet (3.7 m) across. It lives in the deep ocean around Japan. It looks like a really big daddy longlegs spider.

Hermit Crab

Hermit crabs live in empty shells. They will also make their home in other objects, like empty bottles.

Lobsters

Lobsters are crustaceans. They are related to crabs and shrimp. They come in many colors, from greenish brown to orange, and even purple or blue.

Lobster

They have 10 legs that include a pair of large claws. One claw grows bigger than the other. They use their claws to crush their prey.

Blue Lobster

Lobsters never stop growing, but their shells don't grow. Instead, the shell splits along the back, and the lobster crawls out of it. Then it has to hide until the new shell hardens. This is called molting.

Spiny Lobster

European Lobster

Lobsters also have many small "swimming legs" called swimmerets under their body.

Shrimp and Krill

Red Shrimp

Both shrimp and krill live in large groups called schools.

Shrimp and krill are both crustaceans. They have hard shells and long bodies with 5 pairs of legs.

Krill

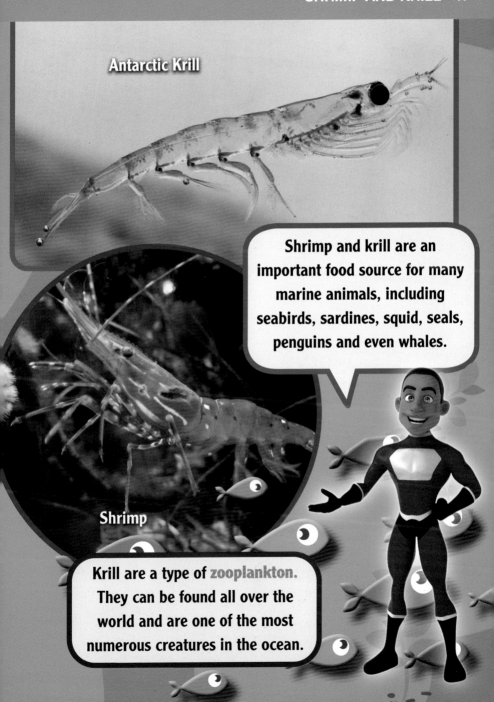

Antarctic Krill

Shrimp

Shrimp and krill are an important food source for many marine animals, including seabirds, sardines, squid, seals, penguins and even whales.

Krill are a type of zooplankton. They can be found all over the world and are one of the most numerous creatures in the ocean.

Seahorses

Seahorses are fish, but they don't have scales. Instead, they have small, spiny plates covering their bodies.

Red Long-snouted Seahorse

Seahorse Rings

They have a backbone but no ribs. Instead, they have rings that go from their head all the way down to their tail.

Seahorses can grab and hold onto things with their tails. They use their tails to anchor themselves to seagrass or coral. Male and female seahorses sometimes join tails.

Seahorse Pair

Pregnant Male Seahorses

The female seahorse lays her eggs in a pouch on the male's stomach. The male carries the eggs until they hatch. Baby seahorses are about the size of an M&M.

Octopuses

The **octopus** is one of the strangest creatures in the ocean. Not only does it have a big squishy head and 8 arms (not tentacles!), it also has 3 hearts, blue blood and 9 brains! Besides the main brain in its head, each arm has its own mini brain.

Reef Octopus

Suckers

The powerful arms are covered in **suckers** that help the octopus stick to things and grab objects. The suckers can also smell and taste! Can you imagine tasting everything you touch?

Octopuses can change color to help them hide when they are hunting or when other animals are hunting them. They also talk to other octopuses by changing color. They can be gray, brown, pink, blue or green.

Common Octopus

Blue-ringed Octopus

The blue-ringed octopus is only about the size of a golf ball, but it has the strongest venom of any octopus. It lives in the tropics and likes to hide in cracks and under rocks.

Squid

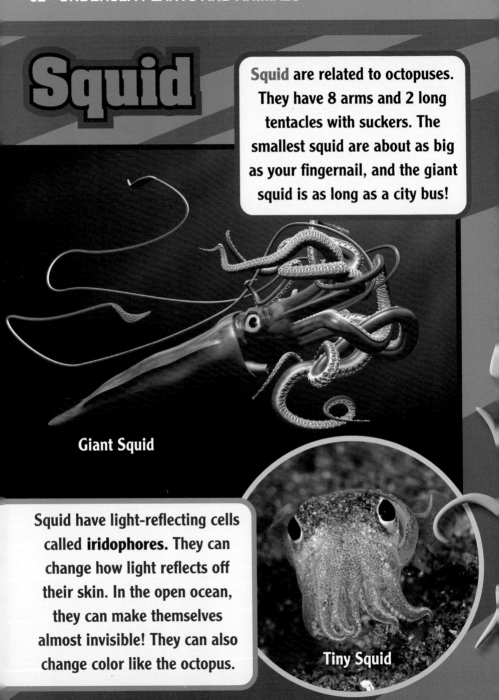

Squid are related to octopuses. They have 8 arms and 2 long tentacles with suckers. The smallest squid are about as big as your fingernail, and the giant squid is as long as a city bus!

Giant Squid

Squid have light-reflecting cells called **iridophores**. They can change how light reflects off their skin. In the open ocean, they can make themselves almost invisible! They can also change color like the octopus.

Tiny Squid

To escape from predators, the squid shoots out a cloud of dark ink. The ink clouds the water and hides the squid so it can swim away.

Bobtail Squid

The giant squid lives in deep ocean water. Its eyes are as big as dinner plates. It can be found in oceans all over the world, but scientists don't know much about it.

Sea Squid

Weird Fish

The **mola mola** looks like a swimming fish head. It weighs as much as a small pickup truck. This fish uses its short tail fin to steer. It is also called **sunfish** because it likes to swim near the surface of the ocean to sun itself.

Mola Mola

The scary-looking anglerfish lives at the bottom of the sea where there is almost no light. It gets its name from the fishing pole that sticks out of its head. The pole has a shiny lure at the end that attracts small fish for the anglerfish to eat.

Ancient Anglerfish

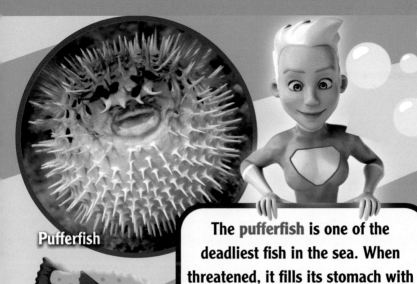

Pufferfish

The **pufferfish** is one of the deadliest fish in the sea. When threatened, it fills its stomach with water and inflates itself into a ball with sharp spines. The poison is in its spines and in its whole body!

The **barreleye** has a see-through head! It lives in the deep ocean. It has telescoping eyes in a clear dome. The eyes usually look up, but they can also look forward.

Barreleye

Rays and Skates

Most **rays** have kite-shaped bodies with whip-like tails that have stinging spines. **Skates** have thicker tails without spines. They are harmless to humans.

School of Rays

Skates and rays are flatfish. Their eyes are on top of their body, and their gills and mouths are on their underside. Their skeleton is made of cartilage instead of bone. They are related to sharks.

Little Skate

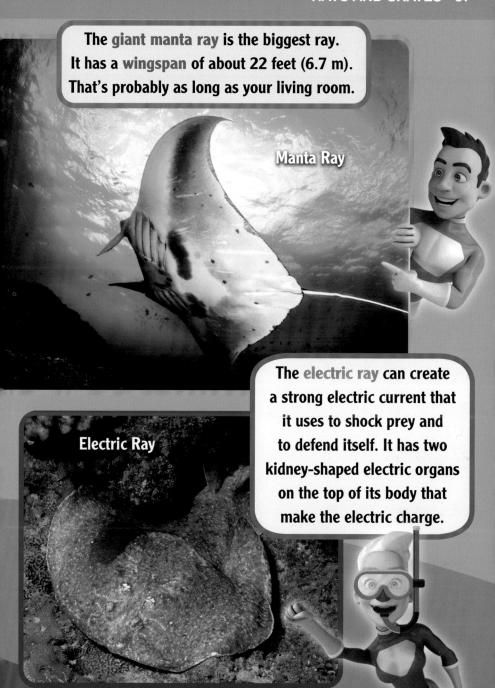

The **giant manta ray** is the biggest ray. It has a **wingspan** of about 22 feet (6.7 m). That's probably as long as your living room.

Manta Ray

Electric Ray

The **electric ray** can create a strong electric current that it uses to shock prey and to defend itself. It has two kidney-shaped electric organs on the top of its body that make the electric charge.

Sharks

Hammerhead Shark

There are more than 300 kinds of sharks, from the giant whale shark that is longer than a city bus to the dwarf lantern shark that's only as long as your hand. Sharks are found all over the world.

Whale Shark

A shark's skeleton is made of cartilage instead of bone. Cartilage is tough and flexible, and is lighter than bone, so sharks can swim quickly without using too much energy.

Bull Shark Teeth

A shark can lose 100 teeth a day! When a shark loses a tooth, a new one moves forward to replace it. Most sharks have 5 to 15 rows of teeth, but the bull shark has 50 rows! A shark can grow 20,000 to 50,000 teeth in its lifetime.

Great White Shark

Shark Awareness Day is celebrated every year on July 14!

Animals That Glow

Some animals glow in the dark. This is called **bioluminescence.** A chemical called **luciferin** helps create light energy in an animal's body.

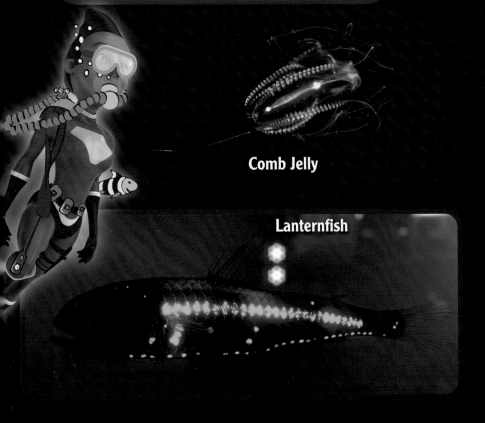

Comb Jelly

Lanternfish

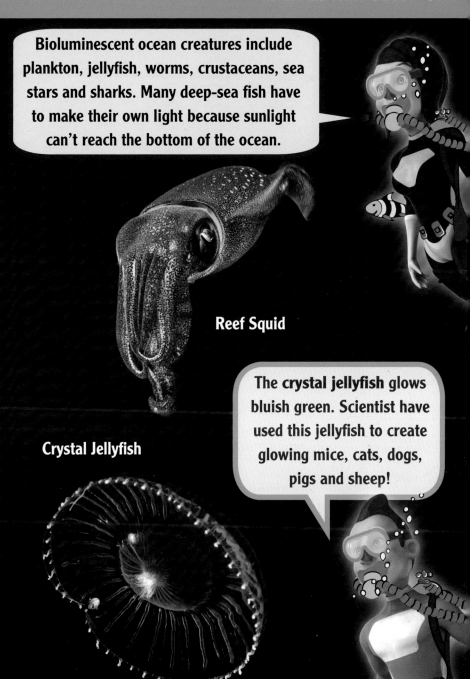

Bioluminescent ocean creatures include plankton, jellyfish, worms, crustaceans, sea stars and sharks. Many deep-sea fish have to make their own light because sunlight can't reach the bottom of the ocean.

Reef Squid

The **crystal jellyfish** glows bluish green. Scientist have used this jellyfish to create glowing mice, cats, dogs, pigs and sheep!

Crystal Jellyfish

Sea Snakes

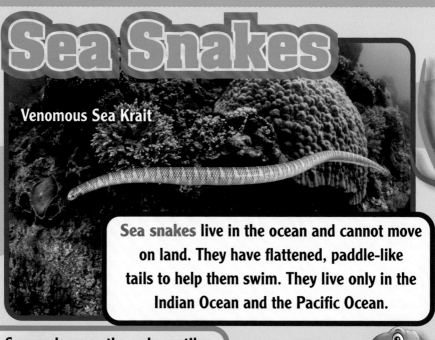

Venomous Sea Krait

Sea snakes live in the ocean and cannot move on land. They have flattened, paddle-like tails to help them swim. They live only in the Indian Ocean and the Pacific Ocean.

Sea snakes are the only reptiles that give birth in the water. The female sea snake stores the eggs in her body. The eggs hatch inside the female, and the young are born alive in the water.

Banded Sea Snake

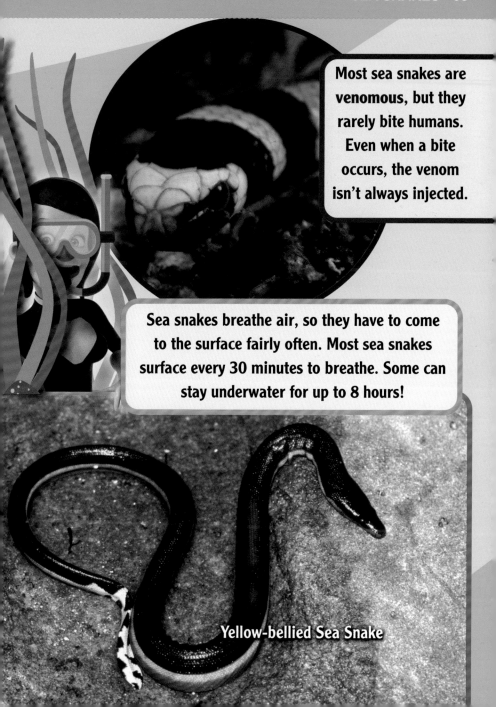

Most sea snakes are venomous, but they rarely bite humans. Even when a bite occurs, the venom isn't always injected.

Sea snakes breathe air, so they have to come to the surface fairly often. Most sea snakes surface every 30 minutes to breathe. Some can stay underwater for up to 8 hours!

Yellow-bellied Sea Snake

Sea Turtles

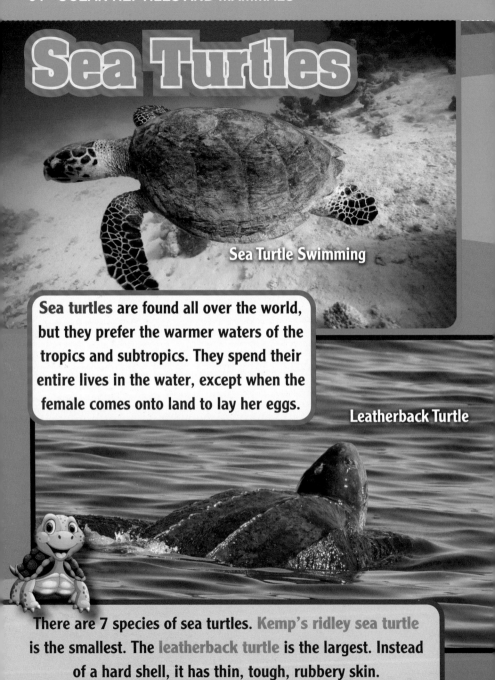

Sea Turtle Swimming

Sea turtles are found all over the world, but they prefer the warmer waters of the tropics and subtropics. They spend their entire lives in the water, except when the female comes onto land to lay her eggs.

Leatherback Turtle

There are 7 species of sea turtles. Kemp's ridley sea turtle is the smallest. The leatherback turtle is the largest. Instead of a hard shell, it has thin, tough, rubbery skin.

Female sea turtles lay their eggs on land. They come ashore at night and dig a hole with their back flippers. After the turtle lays her eggs, she refills the hole with sand and returns to the ocean. When the baby turtles hatch, they crawl into the ocean and swim away.

Baby Sea Turtle

Many sea turtle species are endangered. They are threatened by fishing, poaching, ocean garbage, oil spills, and climate change. Many organizations rescue and help injured turtles and work to protect their ocean habitats.

Young Green Sea Turtle

Sea Otters

Sea otters live along the coasts of the Pacific Ocean from Japan and Russia to Alaska and south to Baja, Mexico. They like rocky coastlines that have thick kelp beds.

Sea otters hunt on the sea floor. They collect sea snails, fish and clams, and store them in a pouch of loose skin on their chest. An otter can stay underwater for up to 5 minutes.

A sea otter doesn't have a layer of blubber to keep it warm. Instead, it has the thickest fur of any animal. Its coat has 1 million hairs per square inch!

Sea otters float on their backs in groups called rafts. Before a sea otter goes to sleep, it often wraps some seaweed around its body so it doesn't float away!

Otter Raft

Seals

Seals are mammals that live mostly in the water. They come on land to rest, mate, give birth or escape from predators.

Harbor Seal and Pup

Seals have flippers instead of feet. The webbed front flippers have 5 fingers with claws. The back flippers help the seal move easily in the water, but they are clumsy on land.

Seals see better underwater than on land. Their large, round eyes see better in the low light of the ocean than the bright light on land.

The largest seal is the southern elephant seal. The male weighs about the same as a hippopotamus. It is also the fattest animal on the planet! This seal lives in the ocean around Antarctica. Its blubber protects it from the cold water.

Male Elephant Seal

Seals are related to bears, skunks and badgers!

Sea Lions

Sea lions are similar to seals but with important differences. Sea lions have ear flaps, but seals just have tiny openings for their ears. Also, sea lions can use their hind flippers to walk, and even run, on land.

Ear flaps

Sea Lion's Flipper

Sea lions live along the coasts and islands of the Pacific Ocean. They like to live in large groups, called colonies.

Steller Sea Lions

They **talk** using barks, grunts, growls, clicks and buzzing noises. They even talk to each other underwater!

Sea lions need to breathe air, but they are expert divers. They can hold their breath for up to 20 minutes! They hunt underwater for herring, anchovies, crabs and squid, which they swallow whole.

California Sea Lion

Walruses

Walruses live in the Arctic and have lots of blubber to keep them warm. They use their sensitive whiskers to find clams, worms, sea snails, crabs, shrimp and sea cucumbers to eat.

Walruses have long teeth called tusks. They use their tusks to pull themselves out of the water and break breathing holes in the ice from below. They also use them to fight other walruses and protect themselves from predators.

Walruses gather in large groups called **herds.** Usually, males and females have their own herds.

A baby walrus is called a **calf.** If a calf is threatened, its mother will pick it up and hold it to her chest. She will even dive into the water to protect it from a predator.

Dolphins

Dolphins are mammals, not fish. They are related to whales. They can stay underwater for a long time, but they must come to the surface to breathe air.

Orcas

The orca, also called the killer whale, is the biggest dolphin. It has the second largest brain of any animal in the world.

The **bottlenose dolphin** is the best-known dolphin. It is famous for being friendly.

Dolphins and whales breathe through a **blowhole** on the top of their head. The blowhole is like your nostrils! When they breathe out, sometimes you can see a spray of water.

Bottlenose Dolphin

Toothed Whales

Toothed whales have teeth. Not all whales do. Dolphins and porpoises are also in the toothed whale family. These whales eat fish, squid, octopus and crustaceans, as well as marine animals, like sharks, penguins, seals and sea lions.

The sperm whale is the largest toothed whale. Males can weigh up to 50 tons (45 tonnes), which is as much as 700 people! Sperm whales can dive really deep and eat giant squid.

Sperm Whale

The **beluga whale** is white and lives in the Arctic. It has a thick layer of blubber to protect it from the cold.

Beluga Whale

Some whales have a special organ in their head that lets them use sound waves to move and hunt in deep, dark waters. This is called **echolocation**.

Baleen Whales

Baleen →

Baleen whales don't have teeth. They have large, bristly plates of baleen that act like a strainer to collect plankton and small fish. Baleen is made of keratin, the same thing that makes up your hair and fingernails!

Bryde's Whale

Right Whale with Baleen

Baleen whales are the largest whales in the world. Bowhead, right, humpback and blue whales are all baleen whales.

Whale Migration

The **blue whale** is the largest animal ever to live on Earth! It is as long as a 6-story building is tall and weighs as much as 33 elephants. Its main food is tiny krill. It has to eat about 40 million krill a day.

The humpback whale is about the size of a school bus and has long, narrow fins. It often propels itself out of the water and splashes back down. This is called breaching. Scientists don't know why the whale does this, but it might just be for fun!

Humpback Whale Breaching

Snorkeling

Snorkeling is a great way to see the beauty of the underwater world when swimming on the surface of the ocean.

A snorkel is a breathing tube that allows a person to breathe air from above the water while they swim at the surface. You wear a snorkel with a mask.

A snorkel also allows a person to make short dives under water, using the little bit of air in the breathing tube.

Scuba Diving

Scuba divers wear a tank on their backs that is filled with air to breathe. They can stay underwater longer and dive deeper than snorkelers.

Scuba stands for Self-Contained Underwater Breathing Apparatus.

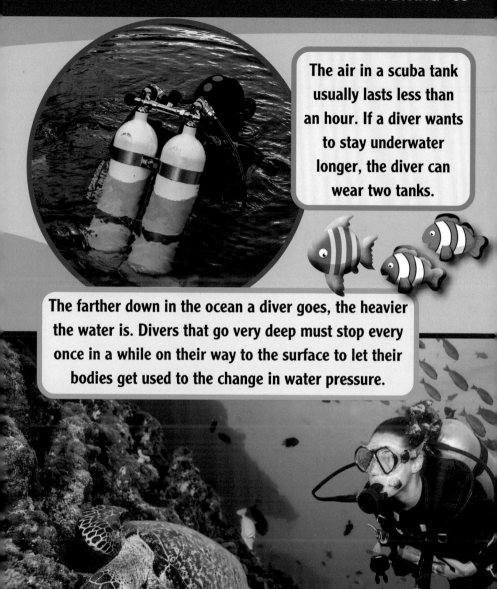

The air in a scuba tank usually lasts less than an hour. If a diver wants to stay underwater longer, the diver can wear two tanks.

The farther down in the ocean a diver goes, the heavier the water is. Divers that go very deep must stop every once in a while on their way to the surface to let their bodies get used to the change in water pressure.

You've probably heard of an astronaut who travels into space, but have you heard of an aquanaut? An **aquanaut** is a trained diver who spends more than a day in an underwater habitat.

NEEMO 16 Crew

Aquarius Reef Base is an undersea research station off the coast of Florida on the ocean floor near coral reefs. Aquanauts spend weeks underwater in the Aquarius habitat.

Aquarius Habitat Exterior

Underwater habitats like Aquarius are laboratories where scientists can do experiments on the specimens they collect from the ocean.

Aquanauts

Ocean Research

Ocean research is important. Scientists study the plants and animals in the ocean. They also study how climate change, pollution and other things affect the ocean.

Scientist Doing Research

Oceanographers study ocean currents, waves, the ocean floor, underwater volcanoes and chemicals in the ocean water.

Some research is done at underwater research stations like Aquarius, and some is done from ships that travel all over the world.

Aquarius Aquanaut

Research Ship in the Arctic

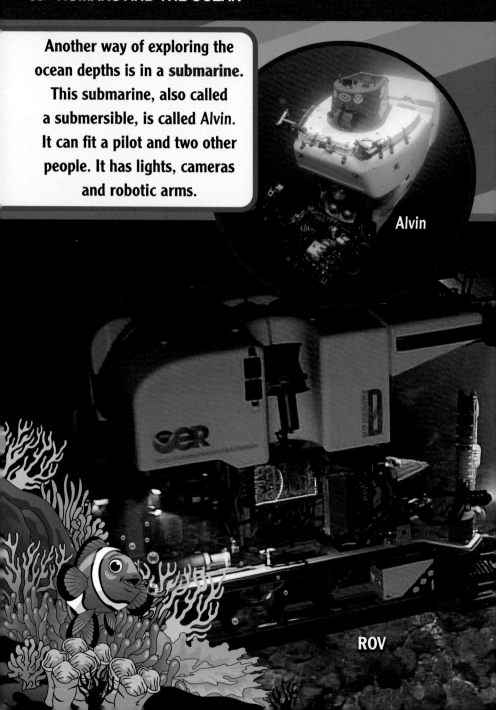

Another way of exploring the ocean depths is in a submarine. This submarine, also called a submersible, is called Alvin. It can fit a pilot and two other people. It has lights, cameras and robotic arms.

Alvin

ROV

Autonomous underwater vehicles (AUVs) are programmed like computers. Scientists give AUVs pre-planned missions that the vehicles do independently.

Sentry AUV

Scientists also use robots to explore the ocean. Remotely operated vehicles (ROVs) are connected to a ship. People on the ship control the robot.

Submarines and Robots

Plastic in the Ocean

It's not just wildlife that can be found in the oceans. When people don't recycle plastic, it can end up in the ocean. Ocean currents create islands of plastic waste far from shore.

Fishing nets make up almost half the waste in the Great Pacific Garbage Patch. It is a huge area of garbage floating in the Pacific Ocean that is about twice the size of Texas.

MICROPLASTICS: TINY PLASTIC, BIG PROBLEM

Plastic can break down into smaller pieces, called **microplastic**. Some animals eat it, thinking it is food. The plastic can make them sick.

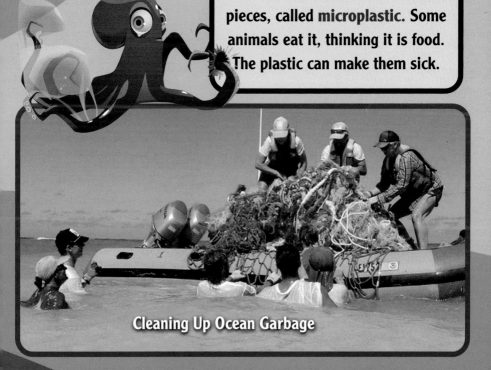

Cleaning Up Ocean Garbage

We can prevent more plastic from getting into the ocean. We can recycle plastic and use things that are made from other materials. For example, we can use glass containers instead of plastic ones to store food.

Also, we can clean up the plastic and other garbage on our beaches before it gets into the ocean.

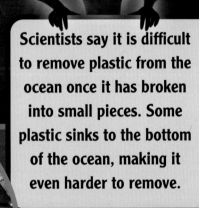

Scientists say it is difficult to remove plastic from the ocean once it has broken into small pieces. Some plastic sinks to the bottom of the ocean, making it even harder to remove.

Keeping Our Oceans Clean

The Future of Ocean Exploration

Recent exploration has discovered many new kinds of sea creatures that have never been seen before.

We still have a lot to learn about the ocean. Scientists know more about the planet Mars than they do about the deepest parts of Earth's oceans.

The future of ocean exploration is exciting!

The Publisher: Super Explorers is an imprint of Blue Bike Books

Library and Archives Canada Cataloguing in Publication

Title: Exploring oceans / Nicholle Carrière, Genevieve Boyer.
Names: Carrière, Nicholle, 1961- author. | Boyer, Genevieve, author.
Identifiers: Canadiana (print) 20220142149 | Canadiana (ebook) 20220142262 | ISBN 9781989209202 (softcover) | ISBN 9781989209219 (PDF)
Subjects: LCSH: Marine animals—Juvenile literature. | LCSH: Marine plants—Juvenile literature.
Classification: LCC QH91.16 .C37 2022 | DDC j578.77—dc23

Project Director: Peter Boer
Design & Layout: Ryschell Dragunov

Front cover: GettyImages-RomoloTavani
Back cover: GettyImages-Michael Zeigler; 3dsam79. Wikimedia Commons-Surtsey eruption 1963.

Superhero Illustrations: julos/Thinkstock.

Photo Credits: KreeftbijDenOsse Bart Braun, 45; Marine_Debris_Removal_...Hawaiian_Islands NOAA.v2, 91; Surtsey_eruption_1963 NOAAv2, 23; Aequorea3 Ssblakely, 61; Atlantic_Ocean_surface, 16; sentry-hires NOAA, 89; Tursiops_truncatus_01 NASA, 75; sikuliaq-hires NOAA, 87; Josef_Schmid_EVA NASA, 87; Aquarius_exterior_(whole) NASA, 85; NEEMO_16_crew_at_Aquarius NASA-Mark Widick, 84; alvin2-hires NOAA, 88; d2-1-hires NOAA, 88; Dumbo_Octopus_(49203817176) NOAA, 19; Phytoplankton_-_the_foundation_of_the_oceanic_food_chain NOAA, 31; ghostfish-hires NOAA, 18; grazers_hirez NOAA, 25; Nikko_smoke_chimnettes smoke_NOAA, 25; Riftia_tube_worm_colony_Galapagos_2011 NOAA,25;

GettyImages: MarinaMays, 53, 51, 48, 47, 44, 45, 43, 39, 37, 36, 34, 33, 10, 18, 26, 29, 25, 32, 56, 63, 67, 70, 72, 73, 81, 85, 84, 67, 55; pleshko74, 55, 51, 46, 43, 38, 36, 34, 24, 11, 9, 7, 5, 56, 60; kuelcue, 38;slowmotiongli, 54, 69, 73,74, 76; Divelvanov, 52; Creativemarc, 49; ginosphotos, 38; scubaluna, 41; Mariusz-W, 46; Andrea Izzotti, 58; Ana Ceciaga Montoro, 37; JumKit, 51; Robert Buchel, 37; cbpix, 41; kateafter, 43; serajace, 39; spyder24, 54; INNA TABAKOVA, 53; AHPhotoswpg, 47; Diane Kuhl, 36; naturediver, 37; LeeYiuTung, 39; Skouatroulio, 42; atese, 57; Whitepointer, 59; AlexRaths, 44; Eduardo Baena, 40; Нина Дроздова, 42; Ja'Crispy, 45; RLSPHOTO, 46; Irina Kulikova, 44; naturediver, 40; heckepics, 43; richcarey, 50; FtLaudGirl, 55; pilipenkoD, 47; sfe-co2, 49; PaulFleet, 52; izanbar, 50; 3dsam79, 55; RLSPHOTO, 53; tane-mahuta, 51; Michel VIARD, 57; Craig Lambert, 49; vojce, 48; Michael Geyer, 58; zixian, 56; s1murg, 59; John Natoli, 56; Agustiawan Agustiawan, 75; jeanro, 66; blueringmedia, 12, 13; sarno sarno, 62; Tigatelu, 22; Dualororua, 65; klyaksun, 90, 91; Eduardo Baena, 68; ThitareeSarmkasat, 94; inusuke, 94; nopponpat, 92; bazzier, 88, 95, 94; m.malinika, 91; RECSTOCKFOOTAGE, 93; Shur_ca.v2, 2, 26; Andriy Nekrasov, 90; Leo Malsam, 83; MaRabelo, 93; VectorMine, 10; Jag_cz, 83; Frogkick, 82; monkeybusinessimages, 92; m-imagephotography, 81;cookelma, 80; bazzier, 85, 84, 86; Daniel Eskridge, 76; solarseven, 79; armiblue, 78; RichardALock, 82; thirtydry, 73; pum_eva, 72; bugphai, 72; GazzaS, 70; pleshko74, 83; Gerald Corsi, 74; MarkMalleson, 79; galitskaya, 81; Gail Salter, 71; Ian Dyball, 69; YULIIA LAKEIENKO, 70; MaslennikovUppsala, 86; Jon Spalding, 68; David McGowen, 66; Eachat, 71; Akhila Easwaran, 65; Alexis Fioramonti, 78; Larina Marina, 90; Ken Griffiths, 63; 3dsam79, 60; Kara Capaldo, 67; CMP1975, 65; jtstewartphoto, 64; maite grau, 69; S_Bachstroem, 95; Velvetfish, 63; RibeirodosSantos, 60; VikiVector, 31, 30, 14, 15; Neil Aronson, 67; Giorgio Cavallaro, 62; atese, 61; panaramka, 90; NaluPhoto, 75; marcinhajdasz, 64; glitterd, 77; Dorling Kindersley1, 77; Velvetfish, 63; mauriziobiso, 70; Damocean, 17; pleshko74, 14, 16; atanasovski; heckepics, 21; fusaromike, 33; Robert Pavsic, 33; joebelanger, 27; Videologia, 30; Mblain93, 35; Oxford Scientific, 19; UWPhotog, 14; OzziesImages, 34; Videologia, 31; tonaquatic, 30; Romolo Tavani, 21; Michael Zeigler, 27; Jennifer Seeman, 34; Chris DoAl, 33; LFPuntel, 7; mychadre, 17; Lemanieh, 35; NicoElNino, 7; Velvetfish, 15; tororo, 6; M-Production, 15; RomoloTavani, 8; avstraliavasin, 6; HenriVdl, 21; Aleksandr Durnov, 8; Colin Rose, 22; scubaluna 28; Damocean, 29; johnandersonphoto, 28, 29; mychadre77, 5; Dorling Kindersley1, 24, 23;

Produced with the assistance of the Government of Alberta.

Alberta
Government

We acknowledge the financial support of the Government of Canada.
Nous reconnaissons l'appui financier du gouvernement du Canada.

Funded by the   Financé par le
Government   gouvernement
of Canada   du Canada

Canadä

Printed in China
PC: 38-1